Payday Loans

Poems by Jee Leong Koh

POETS WEAR PRADA • Hoboken, New Jersey

PAYDAY LOANS

First North American Publication 2007.

http://pwpbooks.blogspot.com

ISBN 978-0-9817678-9-5

Printed in the U.S.A.

Cover Art and Back Cover Photo by Jee Leong Koh.

For W.

*Poets who cope with everyday vicissitudes by saying them
do not tend to produce fully formed, self-standing "poems."
... Rather, it is each one's persistent attitude that is his poem;
the whole book is a more objective poem than any of the poems.*

—Paul Goodman

April 1, Friday

Please lend me thirty, Mr. Certain Death.
In cash. You'll get them back on my payday,
the sum assured, with the levity of breath.
I need the loan right now to make my way.
My boyfriend doesn't want me to move in
yet. I'm leaving school without a job.
My visa is expiring. I begin
again a sonnet when the brain's a throb.
Last night, a Coke-drinking economist
discoursed on lenders jacking up their stall
and interest rate for those desperate or pissed,
spending their days in poverty's deep mall.
The man concluded it's irrational
to borrow from you, Mister, to subsist.

April 2, Saturday

My cipher is the Paradise Tree Snake
which flattens itself into aerofoil
and glides. This house on earth is luck's mistake;
I'm born of air, not water, wood or soil.
Here many snakes exist, less snake than sock.
A python sleeps in its non-Delphic pit.
Two oriental whips knot in wedlock.
And a black spitting cobra does not spit.
This cage has stupefied desire and doubt;
I must escape into the thrashing trees
and navigate in darkness like the scout
who senses through its skin false guarantees
and turns, mid-flight, towards the unforeseen,
not held back by what has, or might have, been.

April 3, Sunday

Love, your apartment is a mess, a state
for six years you live with, in, no, become.
Newspapers, postcards, post-its, bills are crumbs
scattered on this rented hardwood plate.
Floored in the room, the mattress conjugates
the two of us; pajamas glad bridegrooms
remove the morning afterwards assume
an aspect of permanence. Why hesitate
then when I say I'll move my stuff to join
my brief, in that white drawer, and toothbrush?
You say you need your space bought with the coin
of years making the mess your own, the hush
when you can't hear the argument of groins.
My rucksacks wait. They don't, won't, no, can't, rush.

April 4, Monday

To which united state can I apply
for the position of official bird,
or unofficial, when what seems preferred
are local fliers states themselves supply?
And rightly so, Heart twitters in reply,
for countries to prefer what they have spurred
to flight, returning songs that they have heard,
or what adopted like the cuckoo. I,
alas, am not a cuckoo-clock nor bald
two-headed eagle and it is too late
to try to be either, but I have hauled
my famine ocean-distance from the Strait
of Singapore, and quaver to be called,
so I can crash-land at the correct gate.

April 5, Tuesday

Rage, as before, against the Fall, Baghdad,
the body's prick, but in a villanelle?
If style's a way of being in the world, as Good-
man says, against what does the change rebel?
The termite temple of lust, fame and friends?
World closing in like water? From the shore,
the wave outruns and picks three out of ten.
The pope died yester—, no, the day before.
So long, pope! We're still left with Mystery
you poke and jab and slap and kick and hack
while crooning sweetly to her in your shack.
(Here it comes: the obligatory flattery.)
Your twelfth book opens with a tenor's plight,
brings down the house with *entry into night*.

for Stephen Dobyns, on the publication of Mystery, So Long

April 6, Wednesday

Lifeguard, who are you watching in this train
awashed in styrofoam along the aisle?
Your shoulders search me with so bright a smile
that it goes down, through, like a good champagne.
These past months, year, treacherous tides, in vain
I have been waiting for a versatile
Savior to hold me up in dry denial
of waters that have swallowed up Hart Crane.
Save me—your sweatshirt boasts of your vocation
—from love's inexorable throat, a coward
like me who wishes by this invocation
to float and flout the flux. Loose-limbed lifeguard,
what do you have to say? You're on vacation
and this your stop? But there's a huge reward!

April 7, Thursday

[Smacks his head] Of course! That's the secret!
Pulitzer winner and a battery
of awards, Ted Kooser lasts so long as poet
and insurance Prez because of his secretary.
(Think Wallace Stevens.) "Miss Lincoln, take care
of this, will you?" "Where's that file, Miss Lincoln?"
"The last poem, Miss Lincoln, is it quite *there*?"
Give me my loaf-haired secretary. Larkin.
The lucky bastards. Then your voice reminds,
"Do you need this shirt for your job interview?"
and I think I'm the lucky bastard, assured
you'll run my Benefit and Life while I
dictate, your voice efficient on the line
to me. "Yes." President and uninsured.

April 8, Friday

"Poop-on-the-Floor," insult the kids, preschool
in Collins' poem, and "Dumb Goopyhead."
Latino Boy retorts, "This poem's retard,
it's written by a white." Indian Girl rules,
"Nobody talks like that." She wants Abdul
to smile at her or smirk at what she said.
The black boy stares, dreaming, into the yard.
The others give up. Their blank looks are cool.
How do I write for these? They're merely types
within whom roam detachments of girls and boys,
and within them grown-ups, their stars, their stripes,
commanding a terrible allegiance. Deploy
rhythm and rhyme? Send for Rumi? LeRoi?
Reduce to gangsta rap? "Retard," he snipes.

April 9, Saturday

Frank, the Italian, stops the leaving priest
and asks, scissors in hand, "Who's the next pope,
Father?" The cleric smiles, "I've not the least
idea." "Why the mystery? The bishop
of Milan, right? A powerful diocese.
Never Nigeria. He's got no hope."
The cleric leaves a generous tip. Greased,
Frank turns to the two dark barbers, who mope
around the shop, and asks, "You know the poop?"
One nods vaguely. The other says, "I know,
yeah, yeah. The poop." Frank points to his arse, "Poop."
I sit down in Frank's chair and think ("I know,
I know.") about my job interview ("Poop,"
Frank chuckles.) and how Frank's the best I know.

April 10, Sunday

My love is curling dumbbells to his chest
because he thinks I don't love him enough
and since he thinks I don't love him enough
my love is curling dumbbells to his chest.
I turn the page of a flesh mag, obsessed
with groping bodies beautiful and buff.
Groping for bodies beautiful and buff,
I turn the page of the flesh mag, obsessed.
My love is groping dumbbells to his chest
to turn his body beautiful and buff
because he thinks I don't love him enough
since I am curling the flesh mag. Obsessed,
my love is curling as I turn the page,
because he thinks I love a beautiful image.

April 11, Monday

I pound and pound this what-do-you-call-it,
Elliptical, EFX546,
pumping the body all that chemical shit,
shooting morning its new daily fix,
instead of pondering over a new sonnet:
a little song to turn the body cold;
a debt requiring its pound of meat;
a Mini made from an injection mold.
It's true I haven't moved although I've run
3 miles and, like my writing, I'm as far
from what the mind wants and the mirror sees,
and though it's true I pound like everyone
on these mass-produced wheels, my chariot-car
signals I've lost four hundred calories.

April 12, Tuesday

My Kyrgyz classmate, after the revolution,
spoke of his government's overthrown known
to none of us. Either it was not shown
on TV or clashed with *Makeover Solution.*
In a Bel-Air suite, regretting her resolution,
a woman has her thighs sucked thin as bones,
face broken in and reconstructed, breasts blown
to a choice of Ds, endured as absolution.
When she goes home, what does the Head of State,
freshly installed, tell her? What ritual bull
do the new priests sacrifice? The bureaucrats
will do as bureaucrats do. When the wool
is snatched from her eyes, as the women wait,
she feels her face, "Oh my god! I'm beautiful."

April 13, Wednesday

Come on, straight boy, and make gay love with me.
One night of loving will not turn you queer,
if queer is what you will not bend to be.
Loving a man is but a change of gears.
Why do it with a girl, an undulating
waterbed, and stress leaks pinched too late?
Why with an oven she loves regulating,
you stick your tray of cookies in, and wait?
Men love themselves when they love other men;
loving themselves they know well how to give
each other head, maneuver two or ten
round the bend of straightforward relief.
What have you got to lose? Leap, acrobat!
You can always fall back on pussycat.

April 14, Thursday

For years I had been running a low fever:
hot coals heaped by the saints onto my head;
traction from the rutting wheels of an achiever
who minded what in Singapore could be said.
Now freed from church and state, I'm a believer
in the pursuit of happiness instead.
Poetry is my chosen course, the lever
for straightening dislocations in my bed.
You read my work for indiscretions, claim
them yours, to be used only with permission.
Love, are you Priest or Law, another name
for Censor? Or is *my* love in remission?
I will still write like a free man on a lame
excuse: accept me, Love, with this condition.

April 15, Friday

How do I write for these? The student sniped
and the shot's ricocheting in the school
when I return to them their stories typed
to fit what I have taught are fiction's rules.
I am well-trained and train my students well
to distinguish good from bad and right from wrong
as if it isn't difficult to tell
to which embattled camp such things belong.
I am well-trained to devastate dissent,
cut off supply lines, dig in or delay
the enemy, which is why I resent
the sniping of my competence that day.
How should I write for these, when my desire,
Goodman, is to return fire for fire?

April 16, Saturday

Bad start: you searched the Net for me, and loved
an early poem in a style so jeweled
I blushed and stripped it down to a bright nude.
Preferring still the body shod and gloved,
you saw more than I did. How you approved
as I read Proust aloud, of the pulchritude
of blurry windows when the women screwed
each other; vaguely, vastly, you were moved.
Last night I stripped before a cheering crowd
but had eyes only for where you stood,
and then for the train window, still too proud
to ask. You answered in bed, "It sounded good."
Faint praise from the beloved! How loud, how loud
I heard the glass, in virtual space, crack.

April 17, Sunday

I wake up with a hard-on and the light
between the hotel curtains gives the finger,
no rosy morn but pale pleurisied bringer
of the day to come: I'll write to write to write;
we'll see, since we're sight-seeing, the sights;
lunch with an ex-boyfriend not seen in years;
go to a bar where we will lust and leer
but do nothing before we call it a night.
I turn and turn and still the sheets disgust
me. He disgusts me. I disgust me. Lust
disgusts me. And the finger, bruised, a slight
cut in the curtain, previously a smear,
hardens into a direction, clear,
desirable and promising as light.

April 18, Monday

What's on tonight but lips pressed on lips,
the neck, the hollow of the collarbone,
down on the silver strings from chest to hips,
bass guitar counterpointing basement's groan;
and on the stirring cord, lips fawn, and tease,
teeth sheathed, to please and worry its backbone:
an arctic wolf licking the meat it sees,
meat spiked on a knife, the foam its own.
On this white horse, the lancer sits astride.
He jerks the bit and bloods its jaws, care thrown
to the wind, pain spurring the pleasure-ride,
slippery saddle, mounting to one moan—
we come together, separate. Tonight
blunts hunger's edge and whets the appetite.

April 19, Tuesday

This is not a lunch poem. It's an after
lunch poem. I can write this coz I'm jobless.
I've got the afternoon to sit and stare.
This morning I rode the 6 train to Lex
to interview with the School Head. She said
she could sponsor me for an American
visa. I don't remember what my head
said but my heart flew to my stomach. Then
I had a turkey sandwich with grilled
turkey and American cheese, and made eyes
at the huge, blond Latino behind the till.
He looked away. I cruised the park to say HI!
to the gulls. Call coming in. [stops writing]…
It was the Head. I've got a job waiting.

April 20, Wednesday

When angry men made rough rocks beautiful
in Florence or some place where they found work,
they didn't instruct their pupils like a petty clerk
nor inspect hack-hewn stones with a plumb rule.
The teachers sought in future's Istanbul
Byzantium built into the marble's quirk,
and molded to the forms of Greeks and Turks
the breathing figure sat on bed or stool.
I refuse to spend my best and brightest hour
correcting this boy's grammar, that girl's heart,
coruscating like plastic when they shine.
If I'm the model, then let them devour
my passion for highlighting into art
this girl's smooth breast, that boy's vigorous line.

The first line quotes the end of a sonnet by Paul Goodman.

April 21, Thursday

"I dreamed of you last night," my class voodoo-
practicing, commie, vegan, white dyke said.
"I dreamed you were lying stark naked in bed,
stroking the leg without a foot."
Has she confused me with one we both know,
J who graduated last year and treads
heavily on his prosthesis? He's married
and writing full-time. Publishing his first book.
What does the dream mean? Is it an omen?
A curse? A prayer? My wish-fulfillment vibes?
For I've wished, once or twice, to be my friend,
a member of a secret, stoic tribe
that cuts up boys to turn them into men.
I want to be the man the dream describes.

April 22, Friday

Consider this: life is no clinical trial
with safety measures and a control group.
It may give school reports but the whole loop
whistles, if lucky, once in a long while.
So we join studies wishing for the denial
of suffering, wishing not to be life's dupe,
wishing the trials nourish like chicken soup
the nervous heart and make it versatile.
But why fear actions and decisions as though
they are more real than trials? Is it a sham
to say *I'll try my best* instead of *do*?
Not all attempts set out to be a scam.
Even in trials, some who take the placebo
get well. They claim, *I try, therefore I am.*

April 23, Saturday

My father doesn't know Zeus from Zeno
and doesn't care. His philosophy works
through his hard hands, and not through easy talk
(*We have two ears and one mouth.* Robert Koh.)
when he makes the giant a.c.'s fever go
from power plants and when, at home, he checks
his children's tantrums with one palm. He takes
charge, you can say, of climate control. So,
when schoolbooks tell me how these writers dig
their dads in whose furrows they trod and trod,
how for their starry pops those poets burn,
or how yet another posse fights the big
bad artist-paters, Ah! I thank my god,
I am the spark of an electrician.

April 24, Sunday

Because my mother whispered on the phone
so as not wake my sister from her sleep
and face the darkening features of the grown
daughter on whom she banks for her upkeep;
because your father doesn't remember you,
forgets ten minutes after you tell him,
pretends he knows whom he is talking to,
and you, my love, may share his fate and shame;
because we won't have children of our own,
and you or I must be the first to die,
and poems are rich outlay but poor loans
for dying years, good answers but bad replies;
therefore I'll spend my days paying the cost
of work, too poor to gain *Paradise Lost*.

April 25, Monday

May good flowers always bloom for you
And good fortune always be yours too.
The red paper pocket my parents sent
presents six crisp one-hundred dollar bills
they can't afford but will still send until
I'm married or dead. Needing every cent
to pay the cost of New York City's rent
while ambition hustles to fulfill
desire, I don't swindle, steal or kill
but pocket the greenbacks and their portent.
I think of Hart Crane, strongly doubtful, bent
on being a writer, dining on goodwill,
talking up muse and love like, yes, a shill,
and plucking the roses the rich soil lent.

April 26, Tuesday

Frankly, I don't give a shit for spring
poems. *April is the cruelest month*, they say,
or *coolest*. Me, I've never seen the gray
budding to green in brown-toned, -stoned Brooklyn.
The leaves appear overnight on the scene.
Those tulips look transplanted from some bouquet.
They're not mouths. Call them tongues and still they say
nothing. The grass, O, green grass, does not sing
but the birds screech to bits the tall sunshine,
and so down to the promenade I stray,
to see Manhattan's permanent skyline
still missing what has never died away.
No winter there and so no leafy sign.
A sudden mist can hang around for days.

April 27, Wednesday

I can't decide which organic bread to buy,
the pumpernickel or the multi-grain.
The tents of death still fly on flooded plains
and campers pray for drops of food supply.
I can't decide which organic bread to buy.
The fucked-up prisoners-of-war complain.
The pumpernickel or the multi-grain,
I ask the empty counter. No reply
but the new pope speaks out against the tie
of gay marriage legalized in Spain.
The prisoners protest for checkout lanes
and campers pray to satellites that fly
over their heads while I decide to buy
the pumpernickel, or the multi-grain.

April 28, Thursday

I thought being gay saved me from being a man
and man's mistakes: great wall, sacked city, rape
and either/or. Victor or also-ran.
Pope or poop. Beta male or top ape.
Or, in my mind, Poet (upper case) or not.
Last week, before you read, your daughter ran
and tied your hand in hers. You loosed the knot
for a while, and read to strangers, students, friends.
I think of the women who lived, loved and wrote,
those who still do, as someone's daughter, wife
and mum. I'm that male poet who shuts his life,
so he can write, then read his work, and quote
Bradstreet, Dickinson, Smith, Browning, Glück,
Rossetti, Sexton, Moore, Plath, Brooks and Rich.

for Marie Howe

April 29, Friday

At lunch you said you hadn't written much
but nursed your fiancé's sister whose tumor burst.
How could you have done otherwise? Death first,
then babies, suckle as you get in touch
with the Mother archetype. Sure, you're engaged
to a devoted man but he can't breast
feed, can he? Babies are bottles of thirst.
Your words at lunch betrayed no sense of grudge.
Maybe I was too dense. Maybe too glad
I have a dick and not your burdened slit.
I don't have time and patience for the act
of bearing with the world. Never a dad,
I'm free to fuck and run and write of it.
Fuck that. I'll sign the bloody job contract.

for J. E. P

April 30, Saturday

In the first year, you said, a coin is dropped
into a bottle each time a couple fuck.
They take the rest of their lives, seconds copped,
to empty the decanter, with some luck,
coin by long coin. I think of your loose change
tossed into the cup—quarters, pennies, dimes
—silver and copper tokens from a range
of corduroy you wore at different times,
and become sad. Then I recall you would
pick up some coins before we left the house
so as to pay with exact cash for food
I enjoyed as more than friend and less than spouse.
Over the cup, thinking of memory's sum,
I read on a dime *e pluribus unum*.

Acknowledgements

Most of *Payday Loans* was written during the 2005 National Poetry Writing Month promoted by the online poetry workshop, *Poetry-Free-For-All*. For many years, I have benefited greatly from the encouragement and critiques of workshop members and moderators.

For their support in the form of writing residencies and scholarships, I am grateful to the Kimmel Harding Nelson Center for the Arts; Kundiman, directed by Joseph Legaspi and Sarah Gambito; and Soul Mountain Retreat, organized by Marilyn Nelson and funded by the University of Connecticut.

At Sarah Lawrence College, my teachers, Stephen Dobyns, Vijay Seshadri, Marie Howe, and Kurt Brown, showed by example and instruction what a poem is and can be. I am also grateful for their many kindnesses.

www.ingramcontent.com/pod-product-compliance
Lightning Source LLC
Chambersburg PA
CBHW061759040426
42447CB00011B/2373